TABLE OF CONTENTS

Dedication...

Acknowledgement...

Foreword..

Introduction...

Chapter One: You Deserve More Than This

Chapter Two: Be Limitless............................

Chapter Three: Soar! You Are Enough and Able

Chapter Four: The Financial Mojo...................

Chapter Five: Feel Alive Amidst All............

Chapter Six: In The Sky Of Abundance.......

If luck was a ready-made entitlement responsible for the success of superior achievers, everyone would have ever got it and would be highly prosperous; The truth is there is nothing like ready-made luck, Champions make their own luck, luck is made. It is a result of combined-focused efforts towards a purpose, we create luck through applying a change atmosphere by the application of universal disciplines and principles of achievement, happiness and productivity, and these can include, faith, analysis, action, vision, persistence, courage and grit among others. Luck is attracted, luck doesn't not attract anyone. You attract it by being the person who deserves it. Luck is not accidental neither an entitlement, it is something got from toil

Acknowledgement

To all those who have shared their wisdom through writing. That through books, we would learn, find our footing and be able to write more.

My mentors both actively and passively have done a great work to keep me dancing in the rain. Keep your Champion Mojo Burning. I truly acknowledge the support transmitted towards my journey; our journey always.

To God who bestows wisdom, knowledge and understanding to us.

Foreword

Upon reading this book I realized there are so many reasons why we tend to play small in our lives, business inclusive. By playing small, I mean all those times that we dim our light, and run away from the challenges at hand to comfort.

Majority of humanity is indirectly taught essentially not to be too much, not to get too big, not to become too happy, not to be 'too' of anything, to have less grit, to conform to society beliefs, have less curiosity and just fit in. Even though I have grown to break some rules from above situations and establish myself higher, this book has had more to teach me.

This book demonstrates that there is a breed of people that believe that playing small to feel validated and accepted by the convention is a losing game. If we cannot deal with who we really are or desire to become, then we should not claim to have a life of our own.

The Champion's Mojo demonstrated to me that we are capable of so much more only that we choose to scratch surface. We keep letting our success down, sabotaging our systems, delaying our happiness and not leaping financially, emotionally, spiritually and socially.

This book is an open door to an expansive journey towards getting gritty, transformed and re- engineered. So powerful. Looking forward to your transformation. Get the mojo burning.
Salim Ghalib Al Ameri
ConneKt Global. Al Ain United Arab Emirates

Introduction

14th of December 2017 will always remain etched on my heart. Before going to bed the previous night, I had promised myself that I had had enough. With effect from the following morning, the 14th, I would embark on a journey of being a new and better me. I had had enough of the rat race. For the past six months, I had been failing emotionally, spiritually and financially. I had lost my MOJO. A relationship had ended on a toxic note at the same time tables turned in circles I worked. My staff had laid down their tools in some month and misery, stress, debt and worry were strangling me. I had to journey back into the noise of my thoughts.

I had to bring to a halt a number of personal projects I was doing. My books' projects were on hold and all promises to release them were overdue. I had no morale of meeting my work deadlines. I would make appointments only not show up, promise payments only to forget and not fulfill them.

14th was the day I would stop tying myself up in the same old knots and landing up in the same dead ends. Until that day, everything was part of the problem, and everything from then on was a learning experience. I chose to leave any guilt and shame firmly in the past. I promised myself to do

 my best to break away from any negative chain-patterns as I redefined my life. I convinced myself that it was okay to screw up and to cry as long as I did not lead myself to the space I was before. I focused on living, learning, and breaking free. (I call it the LLBF theory in my trainings.)

Tony Robins says, "All greatness starts with failure. When you succeed, you celebrate but when you fail, you ponder and all greatness starts with pondering". That pondering led to the compilation of lessons that is this book. I pray you find the courage to go after what you desire before it's too late. Enjoy your reading.

CHAPTER ONE

YOU DESERVE MORE THAN THIS

"If you don't give away your personal power, no one can take it away from you, you will ultimately discover that your external enemies and barriers are nothing more
compared to the internal; someone said: I have discovered my enemy and the enemy is 'me'." – Praise George

The Transcendence

Transcendence is the act of rising above something to a superior state. We are all born ignorant, with nothing on us. Our purpose of living is to make shifts from one state to another. The most satisfying state one can go to is the Championship state. To be a champion is to have transcended; to being at a superior level. We are all born like rocks and placed in the wilderness, if we stand still, we gather a lot of moss. Champions never stand still. Like a rolling rock, they never allow moss to grow on them. They transcend. Transcendence comes from the Latin prefix *trans-*, meaning "beyond," and the word *scandare*, meaning "to climb." When you achieve transcendence, you have gone beyond ordinary limitations beyond external validation and beyond victimization of daily life situations. To transcend is to soar!

If you have crossed from the victim stage of life to some level of life growth, called independent or hacker stage, then you may agree with me that everyone is gifted and strong only that some of us never open the gift package to the fullest. We become like static rocks and gather a lot of moss on us. At times, we make a few scratches on the ground and run away thinking we have exhausted all there was to be done. As Jonathan Santos says, "Some people even fear shadow-like blocks forgetting that a shadow means there is a light shining somewhere around that needs to be looked up to vigorously with extra effort, extra faith, extra hope, extra time and extra grit."

Growing up, my parents were abject poor. Their poverty was marred with intricacies of untamed domestic violence. My mother was a potter; so loving and caring, and my dad a lumberjack; so toxic, alcoholic and violent. As a result, I was rejected basic freedom several times as early as age 3. I survived being sold twice at the age of 7. Our old little grass thatched house stood on an angle of 45 degrees and often times cheated on the weight of storms to remain standing. At 13, I was the best student at the Primary Leaving Examinations (PLE) only to repeat the class for lack of fees to crossover to secondary school. At 15, I joined junior technical education and studied carpentry and joinery. It was the last time I stayed at home. I left my mother to begin on my own.

My first job was carpentry. I am a professional carpenter. I worked with many companies as a young technical man and later did countless jobs outside carpentry. I gave a shot to a number of businesses before my 20th birthday. Some I succeeded while others I lost.

At 20, a friend and I started a company that enjoyed short term massive success on grounds of poor financial management. Neither of us had any sense of financial management at all. As quickly as the business rose, so it fell with nothing to hold it back. In 2008 at 22, I came to Kampala city on promises of a job. Little did I know that the said job had no pay attached to it.

In 2009, I started a business, in faith, with small capital of UGX 8000 (about USD 3.5 at the time). My goal was to multiply its growth by 1000 times in one year. I made it in the 8th month. In 2010 I started a supply chain company which turned out well.

In 2012, I decided to slow down on everything else I was doing and do something I loved, something that made me serve my purpose for living; marketing, consultancy and Training.

Around the same time, I went back to school.

I was exposed to new ideas that I had taken for granted. I took a forward leap with my marketing skills much as it was something new for me. I easily blended in. Two years later, I had started handling local and global consultancy and training projects.

I have since authored three different titles, consulted and trained for a number of organizations and individuals on top of being a serial entrepreneur. Through it all, I have made mistakes, some that hurt and others that have motivated me to bounce back. I have been corrected and criticized. I have been hurt. I have been forgiven and I have forgiven several times as well.

It is in these experiences where resilience and I began our journey. A journey that led to championship. I never knew the power of resilience and its connection to transcendence. I never really understood what resilience was even when I was experimenting it every other day. I believed that in order to be considered resilient, one had to have reached the summit of the mountain.

Resilient people were distant from me, or so I thought until I reflected on all these circumstances. It's been only after crossing over some bridges that I have come to value and respect the power of resilience in life. Life has a tendency of throwing numerous thorny balls to you making it hard to dodge them.

A number of times, I have felt defeated, humiliated, rejected and useless. However, I have survived, bounced back, and stood again. I am a creative work in progress. The bottom line is; we have the power of choice rather than being at the mercy of chance, possibility or situations. Once you discover the power in you, it works like magic. Like an elastic band, you learn to stretch and fold. You become a sponge that soaks and absorbs every fluid it comes across. This power is transformative. It gives you a new shape. Its transcendence comes with a feeling of power and gratitude I call the **Champion's Mojo!**

In this book, we define a **mojo** as an extraordinary outlook, skill, or drive that spurs you to achieve beyond your limits. Our mojo is the source of magical courage to keep going.

I call it transcendence power. You have it! The power to transcend, the Mojo and the acceleration spark that shifts gears on steep terrain. It is this champion's mojo that results into disruption against friction. Transcendence is equal to time multiplied by the level of resilience and purpose. Transcend!

Time to cause rage and positive disruption

Have you ever wished, prayed or thought you could go to bed on a given night and wake up the following day with no baggage whatsoever? That you would wake up with nothing weighing you down, feeling loved and peaceful without hardships? Until we address them, these wishes are always playing in our mind making us victims of our own thoughts.

It is easy to get lost in the wishful world and not work on bettering self. Such wishes take away our personal power in exchange of fear and frustration. This stops us from evoking a raging revolution within us. This could be the difference between us and the people we admire. These people have seen life as an endless process of rage not as destination of comfort, so they enjoy a day at a time. Instead of wishing, they rev up into action. They disrupt the status quo.

As mentioned in the introduction, at one time my companies and I were in deep debt without any asset, savings or defined income. I had lost it all. I felt so frustrated at my helplessness. I lost money and peace due to the poor decisions, partnerships and networks that I had made. Just when I thought things were getting better, a new wrench would block my plans again until I realized what was holding me back. In brief, I had lost my mojo. As soon as I realized what was holding me back, I sprung up into action and changed it. And this took me some pretty good time. Wow! Life can change too fast. Fast is not about magic but the moment you gain courage.

As a result of a few hacks in my life and regaining my mojo, I challenged myself to make better and informed decisions henceforth. I was out to be who I wanted to be. It is a mental trap, to think that you can do nothing to change the status of how things are. I've been freed from this trap at least just as I have graduated from the victim stage to being a freethinking character. This is not to say that I am well off or immune to struggles or that I have attained high level success or seen the pinnacle of my dreams but when I look back at the depth of the pit from which I have emerged, I have the guts to say, "Wow, I made it".

We all need our mojo; our magic— our very best energy—to run our business, to lead our teams, to talk to our clients, and to be the best champions we know we can be. As Maya Angelou says; "Without courage, we cannot practice any other virtue with consistency. We can't be kind, true, merciful, generous, or honest." It's so true that when we lose our mojo, we lose the courage and audacity to live. When we question ourselves, when we trouble ourselves with doubt, the mojo helps us do the things we need to.

There comes a moment in life when the life you are living feels too small for who you are seeking to become. You realize you deserve more. You venture out to defy the odds. In doing so, you keep your mojo aflame. You choose to outgrow your circumstance and become a better version of you. This is the only time you can achieve the unimaginable. This moment is very powerful much as it is scary. It requires you to let go of your former self to become a new you.

When you find yourself at the bottom of a valley, consider that the universe is clearing away whatever is not in alignment with your highest good and making space for your bigger blessings. In such times, life invites you to grow, reinvent yourself, evolve and become an authentic you. The only ticket you can use to honor this invitation is keeping your mojo on and burning.

Whether it is a relationship, job, business or a project, the courage to change situations is the best of all. Even when you are no longer able to change a situation, you are challenged to grow yourself to being a better you. See, it takes time to become the person we really want to be but a champion's role in this time is not a passive one. So how do you keep active?

Do Not Let False Beliefs Downsize Your Dreams and Potential

When I was 11, my mother brought a very nice looking fish from the market. Upon tasting the yummy meal, I threw back. This marked a four day battle with malaria which I had not known prior. As a little boy after healing and looking at how many times my little butt had been pierced with injections, I resolved never to eat fish again. Never and not again was my great resolve.

I believed that it was the fish which had made me fall sick. I never tasted fish for nine years. At about twenty, my peers influenced me to try it again. The fish was so yummy and I did not fall sick again. I had missed out on this delicacy for a whole nine years.

Today, fish is one of my best dishes. The bottom line from this experience is that beliefs are notions and assumptions formed in our minds regarding ourselves and our surroundings that we perceive as absolute truth. They are usually based on emotions and are often psychological and irrational. We get them from religion, culture, parents, environments, pain, etc. This calls for questioning a number of things that we believe in. Minus natural and legal laws, everything else can be questioned. False beliefs limit and control us denying us a chance of exploring opportunities around us.

For example, if you have a belief that mistakes and failure are bad, then you'll avoid many growth and learning experiences. You have to be willing to fail in order to build new skills. If you believe that rejection is a bad thing, you'll avoid approaching new people. There is no progress where false beliefs exist. Don't let false beliefs downsize your dreams and potential.

Centre Your Strength to Your Mission, Not Your Obligations

Once you get lost in a cycle of obligations, you lose touch with your motive and that is the beginning of depression. If that happens, it's time to stop and focus on your mission. Many times, I found myself tied in obligations, missing meetings, falling off my own shadow till I refocused back to my mission. Why are you doing what you do? What's the motivation behind everything you're doing? If you can find your mission, you'll get back your motivation, and if you get back your motivation you will find your confidence and courage to achieve the unimaginable and keep the mojo on. It is only when you are on the right lane of your mission that you can catch up with your obligations.

Do Not Tire From Widening Your Perspective

Sometimes you may feel like you're stuck between two concrete walls where nothing seems to be working. But have you been trying new things, or just variations on the same things that you already know don't work? These are honest questions I never wanted to hear when I was stuck in the trenches and I am certain so many people don't want to hear of them. To shift your perspective and regain your mojo, try doing new things or keep doing old things but in new ways. That calls for a change in your perspective of life. Changing your perspective can help you to renew your confidence.

Learn To Celebrate Small Wins Each Day

Some time back I called a friend over for a celebration upon being accepted for an online course. To them, it was so minor an achievement to deserve a celebration.

They might have been right but one secret to achieve more in life is celebrating your achievements both small and big. This is how one cultivates an attitude of gratitude.

When I was wallowing in the misery of misgivings, I subscribed to *Omvana App* by Mind Valley on using guided meditation as a therapy for healing. One of the key factors that this meditation teaches is to be happy at all times. By appreciating something as small as a cup of coffee would lead me to closing a business deal. Keep in mind that championship is not a one night event. It is a series of repetitive acts. Yet in all that you do, remember to celebrate all your wins however small. Celebrating and being grateful for small wins, restores love, makes it easy to forgive and creates a state of flow and calmness in your career, business and relationships with people.

Champions Are Brave People Unafraid Of Asking For Help

Dear friend, if there's anything good about a crisis, it's that it can help you break the feeling that you have to know, do or be everything. Sometimes the simplest act of asking for help can be the biggest booster to keep your mojo burning. Speaking with someone can remind you of who you really are. Even the smartest, the most successful, most accomplished people need the assistance and support of others at all times. Asking help builds grit.

Eliminate Procrastination on MITs

By far, the biggest confession I can make and which 90% of the population could boldly identify with is procrastination. Procrastination is the avoidance of doing a task that needs to be accomplished. It is the habitual delay of starting or finishing a task despite its negative consequences. Procrastination is a universal human habit that champions have always dealt with. Procrastination and championship cannot live in the same space. Always remember to prioritize the **most important tasks (MITs)**.

Mind fit hypnosis defines procrastination as the practice of carrying out less urgent tasks in preference to more urgent ones, or doing more pleasurable things in place of less pleasurable yet important ones, and thus putting off impending tasks to a later time. Most times in my struggles I have learned a simple lesson: You can look extremely productive without producing anything at all. As Denzel Washington says:

> Just because you are doing a lot more does not mean you are achieving a lot more, movement cannot be confused with progress.

In the name of planning, smartness and identifying of who we are, we procrastinate. We expect things to magically fall in place because we have thought about them forgetting the opposite is true.

My spirit tells me you know what I am talking about. The truth is, you don't make a difference by contemplating. A difference is only made by doing, not talking. I love the motto of Lubiri S. S, *We learn by doing*. It is better to stop drifting and start doing. You don't have to worry about doing it perfectly, or having it all figured out because that may not happen.

Give yourself permission to be imperfect and get better day by day. I gave myself permission to start writing books. I didn't mind my imperfections. One publisher advised me to quit authorship. My first book had every mistake you could ever think of but I kept going. I got better with every other passing day. So, as a champion to crack down unnecessary cultural rules and soar you need to stop procrastination and give yourself permission to be humanly imperfect. Do things and adjust along the way. Remember corrections are done on attempted or wrongly 'done' work not on thoughts or ideas.

CHAPTER TWO

BE LIMITLESS

"If you always put limits on everything you do, physical or anything else. They will spread in your work and into your life. There are no limits. There are only plateaus, and you must not stay there, you must go beyond them."
_____ Bruce Lee

Build resilience. Be Unfuckwithable

Unfuckwithable: a Definition

When you're truly at peace and in touch with yourself. Nothing anyone says or does bothers you and no negativity can touch you.

The word 'Unfuckwithable' is said to have started appearing many times on the internet around 2015. Unfortunately, I could not track down the composer of the term. It commonly appeared in form of an image, explaining what it is. I first had of it from the *middle finger project* blog and later read it in some books. In his book; *The code of the extra-ordinary mind* – Vishen uses the term often times making it more loved and easier to use. When you first hear of the word unfuckwithable, you get the impression the word is of the absurd lineage of the f**k word. Yet it is about somebody who generally doesn't give a damn to mediocrity. When you are unfuckwithable, it means nothing whether problems, people or circumstances can just f**k around with you and take away your personal power. To be unfuckwithable means to know what you want and going out to make things happen.

To be unfuckwithable means having the attitude and thick skin that is unrepentant for being different or for being a go getter. When they say you are an unfuckwithable person, it means you are the kind that creates opportunities for yourself without waiting for somebody else to hand them down for you. Inevitably some time life burdens us with so much weight that we just can't be able to carry. You and I need to be unfuckwithable like this legendary champion.

The Story of Lee

Growing up amidst humble beginnings in the culture quoted Hong Kong, he was taught in the ways of traditional martial arts. At that time, it was against the rules to stray from the traditional teachings of martial arts. However, Lee never allowed anything to limit him, be it in martial arts or life. He went on to invent *Jeet Kune Do*, a hybrid fighting style based on his philosophies of being limitless. Many of his achievements came from his ability to overcome limits. As the founder of *Jeet Kune Do* and a master of martial arts. He became one of the most revered people in the world. And he did all this at a time when the Chinese were still stereotyped as house servants and railroad workers.

He hacked culture and cracked some codes by all means. His dynamism on screen gave him audience appreciation across cultural divides making him one of the most memorable movie legends of the 20th century. He was unfuckwithable to say the least.

We all know Bruce Lee as a major action-movie star and one of the greatest martial artistes in the world. What we do not know is the story of the a thousand and one hills he had to climb to achieve his dream. Bruce Lee accomplished his dream in his early thirties just before his untimely death.

The Trial

He started taking martial arts seriously when he was beaten up by a local gang at the age of 13. He quickly became adept at martial arts as one of the best street fighters in Hong Kong. On a downside, this got attention from the police as well. When Lee beat up one of the boys who was the son of a feared Chinese mafia member, they started fearing for his life and decided it was best for him to get away from Hong Kong and send him back to San Francisco where he was born.

Bruce Lee left for San Francisco where he did odd jobs while studying philosophy at university. He also started holding martial arts classes. It is here that he met Linda Emery, one of his students who later became his wife. At a time when there was considerable opposition to interracial relationships, Bruce Lee and Linda started a relationship and got married three years later.

At the time, many of the Chinese martial artistes disliked him because he was violating their code of culture.   As a result of his code cracking, a martial artiste named Jack Man Wong challenged him to engage in a fight. The conditions of the fight were that if Lee lost, he would close his schools or stop teaching non-Chinese people. If Jack lost, he would quit teaching. Within one-minute Bruce defeated Jack and thus continued to impart his knowledge to everyone who wished to learn.

Becoming a Champion

Bruce Lee had two major career goals both summarized in being extra ordinary. His first goal was to become one of the greatest martial artistes in the world. He accomplished this very early in life. By the time he was in his early twenties, his martial arts skills had already become legendary. He did not only beat the masters but also won every street fight he took part in. He exhibited his skills in many martial arts competitions where he demonstrated his incredible talent.

Bruce Lee's second major goal was to become an action movie star. Accomplishing this was much more difficult but his commitment and participation in many recorded fights led him to being invited for the audition of a TV series called the *Green Hornet*. The show was very successful and Lee's skills were so more phenomenal than those of the lead actor. When the show was aired in Hong Kong, the popularity of Lee's character led the show to being renamed *The Kato Show*.

Failure and Frustration on global breakthrough

Even after the success of the massive show, things would not come easy for Bruce. No matter where he tried to be a lead actor whether for a show or for a martial arts movie, they would turn him down because he was not white. This happened continuously. During this period, he made many guest appearances on many television shows and taught martial arts to some of the leading movie stars of the time. They all were awed by his talent and believed he could be a great star but somehow things never worked out for him. Like any other worthwhile dream, he faced a lot of criticism, embarrassments, rejections and failure.

In 1969, *The Green Hornet* aired its final episode and Bruce was trying to find another television role. Bruce pitched a *Kung Fu* series to the Warner

Brothers who gave him a chance to prove himself. Unfortunately for him, they selected, David Carradine a Caucasian actor, who did not even have as much a martial arts background as Lee. It's rumored that Bruce was never considered for the main role because viewers were assumed not be ready for Bruce's "oriental" looks.

It was a clear case of Hollywood's xenophobia. Like any other road to championship, he was belittled and frustrated but he believed in himself and unfuckwithably kept shining in his brilliance. This is the limitless part of a champion.

Angry, Bruce sat down one night and wrote a letter to himself.

By 1980, I will be the best-known oriental movie star in the United States and will have secured $10 million dollars... And in return, I will give the very best acting I could possibly give every single time I am in front of the camera and I will live in peace and harmony.

Around this time when things couldn't get any worse Bruce Lee injured his back and was bedridden for 6 months. Doctors told Bruce he could never kick again. He adamantly refused to buy the idea. After 6 months, he had barely recovered when he showed up again. Still acting opportunities eluded him. Frustrated, he decided to go to Hong Kong with his family for a short break.

The struggle finally ends: Lee became a Star

To his surprise, in Hong Kong he was recognized on the street by most people as the star of *The Green Hornet* which had been renamed *The Kato Show* due to his immense popularity. Knowing that Bruce was an actor, one of Hong Kong's leading producers (Raymond Chow) asked him to star in a motion picture he was making in Hong Kong, called *The Big Boss*.

The Big Boss was a massive success and turned Bruce Lee into an overnight major movie star in Hong Kong. He followed it up with *Fist of Fury* which was an even bigger hit and *Way of the Dragon* co-starring Chuck Norris which elevated Bruce Lee to an iconic status in East Asia and many other parts of the world. The Warner Brothers came back to him and proposed making a movie that would be released in America as well. It was titled *Enter the Dragon*. This movie would make Bruce an International Star and one of the greatest movie legends of the 20th century. Unfortunately, just days before the release, Bruce Lee passed away of cerebral edema.

Bruce Lee was surely unlucky that he did not get to enjoy much of his success but his legacy carries on many years after his passing. At the end of the day how you impact others matters more than how long you live when you are limitless and unfuckwithable. Bruce Lee was of the rare breed of champions that everyone can draw lessons from.

What drove Bruce to do so much at such an early age? What was his mindset?

Bruce never remained idle or wishful. He never considered himself a master, but rather a student master, who was always eager to learn more about his craft. Here are some lessons we can learn from him:

1) The art of being unfuckwithable requires an incredible work ethic

Bruce Lee became the greatest martial artist not just because of his incredible talent and unfuckwithable attitude but also his great work ethic. Many reporters and friends say he rarely ever missed a workout. If you desire to get better in your field you have to commit yourself to training and doing whatever you need to do to improve your skills. Champions enjoy the state of being uncomfortable always.

2) Always keep learning and trying to get better

Bruce had a voracious appetite for books. Many journalists who visited him say his personal library contained over 2,000 books from various disciplines. Besides martial arts books, Bruce read personal development books from authors such as Napoleon Hill, Dale Carnegie and many more. He never saw himself as a master of anything. He told people that he had skill in the martial arts, but he was still learning, and that was true with his own personal development as well. He continued to expand his knowledge and to grow himself personally.

3) Never give up and overcome the obstacles

As the story reads, Bruce had to overcome some major obstacles on his path towards personal success. He had to overcome poverty, racial prejudice, prejudice within the Chinese community, financial woes, injuries, and lost opportunities. Anyone of these obstacles could have easily erased Bruce Lee from popular culture, but it was his die-hard commitment not to let himself give up that made him the person he turned out to be; limitless and unfuckwithable.

Conquer the Fear Within- You Are Able

Many years ago, a number of my colleagues and I hoped, prayed and believed for change in life without understanding the laws that govern change. For years, we anticipated and believed for wonderful things to happen in finances, business and life in general but nothing significant happened until we learnt of the law of change. The law of change is clear that nothing changes until an external force or action is attracted by a collaborative internal force – all great things start from within

This is what Mark and Angel Chernof said,

> Don't let your life desired moments slip through your fingers by living in the past or for the future. Freedom starts in the present. The past offers no freedom other than threat-based predictions. Living life one day at a time helps you to live ALL the days of your life. This is not to say to forget yesterday or not plan for tomorrow but it's giving yourself permission to be happy day by day. Don't give up when you still have something to give. Don't stop to love when you can still, let not yesterday dominate today and let not today be traded petty for tomorrow. Nothing is really over until the moment you stop trying. But above all, don't be afraid to admit that you are less than perfect. It is this fragile thread that binds us together authentically.

Losing a champion's mojo starts with having fear and when you fear, you lose the emotional and physical resilience. Fear has a place in our entire life, and it shows up daily. Everything causes it: finding new work, dealing with financial uncertainty, creating something new, contemplating failure.

By necessity, our minds are designed to let fear in. Without it, we'd never survive. But then how do you keep fear from impeding your ability to achieve the unimaginable. Conquering fear is about self-awareness, wisdom, and understanding your strengths–often in the face of adversity. You can practice and cultivate these personality traits, thank goodness, and it even gets easier over time. I can't claim that I am a master of this thing called fear, every one fears but I must say I have earned the right to talk about fear and how to conquer it through my experience and I share some key nuggets here.

Basically, to effectively get over fear and be deserving you must tap and make use of the 4 unique human gifts; awareness, imagination, conscience and independent will. Awareness is the ability to know who you are and your surroundings, imagination is vision and conscience is the ability to quickly analyze and tell right from wrong. Independent will is the ability to make decisions with less external influence. When you put to use these gifts then you can and deserve to be a champion. But also, as said earlier; ask why.

Let the 'Why' Question lead you

Why did you start, why are you reading this book, why did you start that business, date that cutie, choose that job, etc. Let the *why* in mind motivate you. I mean the purpose. Acting fearlessly often means heading into uncharted territory, challenging conventional paths, or putting aside the need for safety and comfort. Where do you get the energy to do so?

Usually from your personal calling in life; - usually I insist that purpose must be accompanied by 2Ps which makes it the 3Ps theorem as I always teach it in our Legacy Pearls trainings. It is always PURPOSE, PROCESS AND PROFIT with a bonus of PLEASURE, we describe more in our *"Limitless Courage to succeed"* Seminar.   An Indian philosopher; Patanjali said,

> When you are inspired by some great purpose, all your thoughts break their bonds. Your mind transcends limitations, your consciousness expands in every direction, and you find yourself in a new, great, and wonderful world. Dormant forces, faculties and talents become alive, and you discover yourself to be a greater person by far than you ever dreamed yourself to be.

Should I add on? No. Ensure your purpose is guided by the other 2Ps mentioned above. It makes the damn struggle easier.

Don't Wait For Luck, Create It

As a result of ignorance and conventional beliefs, we think celebrities and high-level achievers found luck. The reality is they created it, they learnt so early the stages of growth and fulfilled the principles fully at each stage through practice, resilience, faith and action. They visualized their future and invented their way into it. Dennis Gabor, in his book, *Inventing the Future*, writes:

> The future cannot be predicted but futures can be invented. It was man's ability to invent which has made human society what it is. The mental processes of inventions are still mysterious. They are rational but not logical, that is to say, not deductive.

Understanding exactly what we want is the foundation for our success. But executing that success requires taking the next step, every day, no matter how difficult it may be. That means you don't sit around waiting for luck but you create it and its resting space. If luck to you is rain that falls to the blessed (contrary to what I know it to be) then still it needs a good place to fall on. Create that. Predict it by creating it.

Do Things That Others Don't Do. Be Unpredictable

Take unconventional paths. Achieving the unimaginable and being a champion requires taking risks for a greater reward (spiritual, financial or otherwise). It takes courage to act different. Fearless people are decisive – the unknown shouldn't paralyze you. You have got to take the road less travelled. I recall when we had to send one of our prayerful clients a Happy Saint's day message other than the conventional festive card, this made him feel so special. He called us the following day in thanks but also with another project. You have got to do what others don't do to keep your mojo on. It's so common for people to crowd around important people at functions after their talks, no one walks to them in their time of comfort. When you struggle to share your contacts in that pool, evidently, your card and message will just fall into a pool of others and they will forget about you. But what if you took the road less travelled and walked ethically to their seat and addressed your need before everyone else? You guessed it right, you would be recognized and considered. Take the road less travelled always and do things that others don't do often. Be extra ordinary.

Like A Steel Bar, Bend but Don't Break

To be extra ordinary calls for fearlessness. Because if you are, you'll develop a mental capacity that lets you adapt, with ease, when things don't go your way. Like steel, resilient people bend but rarely break. You also have to bend but don't break. This sometimes means to let go of the past and start afresh or re-design plans. That ability to let go or redesign drives a constant process of change. It's what makes people flexible and adaptable. Don't be like a block of cast iron that just breaks. Bend but don't break in whatever you do. I have learnt it the hard way that this is actually a great principle of happiness in relationships and business. Try it and make it your mantra.

Turn Every Obstacle into an Asset

In mid-January 2016, while waiting for my connecting flight to Abu Dhabi at Addis Ababa Airport, I happened to read a post on *HuffPost* that changed my mind. It was a story of how Nelson Mandela, in his teens, heard a tribal elder say, "These are our young men. They are our future. But the truth is they are second-class citizens...they will always be boys." Hearing that (obstacle to his beliefs) Mandela decided to change South Africa at an instant. And his decision changed the world many years later and made him one of the greatest leaders of all time. The obstacle of feeling humiliated being called a second-class citizen propelled him to change. Fearless people work with what they have and turn obstacles into opportunities/assets. They are at ease with challenges, disappointments, embarrassments and rejections. Instead of setbacks, they try to see these events as gifts and find ways to utilize them to move forward.

For every tough moment of our past, also needs to come the belief that "I can do it because I have gotten past challenges that seemed impossible." Those past experiences strengthen me because I know the importance that resilience had. It is important however as well, to realize that it is possible to continue taking active steps to become more resilient, you are going through an interview to the greatest position you desire

Learn Life's Glorious Interview

Well, when we talk of interviews, people run away. I once attended an interview for a certain project and my fellow competitors were complaining. They wished they would only be enrolled without the interview process. You may be qualified or deserving but once you don't pass the test on the interview day that will mark the end of you. No wonder we go to offices and find people in positions we think they are unfit for, the secret is they passed the interview when the smart guys were drifting. Interviews are not about intelligence but mainly about courage, strength and drive one has. It's not bribe as often implied. Trump, Mandela, Obama and etc. are not the smartest presidents but they have passed the political interviews and such is life. Well, the whole interview process is about answering the question: "Why should we hire, give or entrust you instead of one of the many other well-qualified applicants?" As it is in hiring and recruiting, every interview question is an attempt to gather information to inform a hiring decision. The same applies to life; every situation you go through is gathering information to qualify you. Both in life and career, either passively or actively you will be asked to convince that you deserve a position.

Why should you be hired? Why are you the best candidate for it among millions who yearn for it? What would you bring to the position once given to you? All these question your intention. To close a business deal, sale or get a great favor in life, you MUST be prepared to be the chosen one. We call this describing your purpose. Remember the give and take principle works everywhere though it's used logically. You must have a passive or active value proposition in order to get something. God gives when he expects a return in many other ways and as well you must convince Him why you deserve something. You cannot attract wealth with no reason as to why you need it in mind. It's a natural principle and law. Even if your interviewer (not seen most times, unless for jobs) doesn't ask one of these questions in so many words, you should have an answer prepared.

Whichever force or powers that be; their interest is to give or favor or hire the best person for the position. The person who has and will show (not one who only has). Truth be told, most of the people that make it to the interview or race at participation stage are qualified for the big win. The winning candidate must be more than qualified, especially in a very competitive market. Remember every hire is a risk for the employer. To God, every favor or provision is risk, you have seen many who were given money and wealth only to use it against the provider! At that rate, His risk was not well calculated I guess (Wink). The provider always takes a risk in recommending a particular candidate to achieve. If the candidate performs well, Mr.

Provider looks brilliant and gets a pat on the back (and maybe a bigger annual bonus in different forms). If the candidate turns out to be a dud, the interviewer looks like a dummy and his reputation suffers in all aspects. That's why it is important to know that even the provider wants to feel important after giving you. You have got to use your position to make his job easier thus;

This principle applies in relationships, work, business and general life. Your answer— whether direct or not- should summarize the top best reasons to hire you. This is an opportunity to reiterate your most impressive strengths and/or describe your most memorable selling points, tailored to align with the description of what you want. These include: experience, Technical skills, Soft skills, Key accomplishments, awards/accolades, transformative milestones/training, accomplishments and success stories are always good bets, especially if you can describe how these demonstrate a desired competency.

My point here is; nothing is by accident. You must pass the interview. There must be a unique combination of attributes that you possess; it may be an attitude, character, deportment, etc. You must look into yourself and truthfully tell the provider that you have all of the skills and experience that they are looking for. It's not just the background of I am handsome, beautiful, I know, I am pretty, I studied or I am worthy, you must also be passionate and driven to answer all life questions and be the person who deserves.

There are people that believe their beauty is their identity to greatness only to end up broke, spoilt and frustrated. No one is too pretty to be broke. Life offers not by beauty but your why and the ability to showcase it in actions, communication and courage. You must have a lot of confidence and be able to concisely sum up how you meet the position's (dream's) top requirements.

Be Alive and Live!

Why do freestyle rappers, authors, hikers, acrobats, mothers, dancers, performers, speakers, preachers, entrepreneurs, musicians, athletes and actors, get beyond natural limits and perform as if supernaturally possessed? They all work with a flow. They are one with themselves; alive and live.

Every champion finds that the greatest moments of fulfillment in life tend to line up really well with the moments in which they have lost all track of time and space. They tend to get lost in the limitlessness of the now. Athletes who tap in the flow, lose the weight and run like ostriches. Musicians like Whitney Houston lived in the flow losing themselves to tap into the magical tunes of the voices. Finding your flow is the super magical secret to achieving the unimaginable.

It starts with you finding the flow. If I may ask; at what point in your recent adult life have you felt genuinely fulfilled and happy for long? If you have been so, you realize those moments you are fulfilled and happy are so glorious. It means you are working in the flow. For some people, it may happen when they're working. For others, it may happen when they're spending time with people. For some, it may come when they're engaged with in a hobby.

I find that the greatest moments of fulfillment in life tend to line up really well with the moments in which I've lost all track of time, space and self. When I'm doing something that I'm so immersed in that time ceases to move. At that moment in life, the watch is still. To get back in the "where did the hours go?" mood. This is what I call flow. The secret of achieving the unimaginable.

That is the peak state of living happily; that moment when you're so engaged physically and/or mentally with something that the constraints of your past just kind of disappear. You're lost in the experience of the moment. That's incredibly joyful.

For me, it happens sometimes when I'm writing or planning for a book release, training or mentoring session. It happens sometimes when I'm one with nature. It happens sometimes when I'm doing things for my daughters. It happens sometimes when I'm reading. It happens sometimes in the midst of a great conversation with a thoughtful friend or two that I talk and feel like not pausing. It happens sometimes when I irreligiously pray or meditate with my soul. It is that moment when I am in flow that I write things and wonder how I got the ideas. Take the example of books, no one ever has words showing on a screen to type, it is after getting into the flow that you discover the hidden treasures, wisdom and strength in you. Flow is *bae* for super achievers!

What do you need to do to maximize the amount of time you spend in that kind of flow state to be alive and live? We have a complete program at Legacy Pearls Africa that will help you do a self-consciousness engineering process and identify the hacks and codes to tap to this with ease.

To me, that's really the answer to what I have fought for in life, something worthy to do with my life- it is the answer of all super achievers we see and wonder how they made it. I am focusing on a life where I have as many of those flow state moments as possible, where my mind, heart, and soul are so engaged with something that I lose track of time. Where distractions and physical and emotional pain get lost in doing whatever it is that's in front of me due to my deep love for it. Find your flow state, do it and live it.

Everything in your life that isn't connected to that sense of "flow" should be enormously secondary to you. You should strive in every way possible to minimize the time, energy and money you commit to those things. If dancing doesn't bring you to a flow state like me, look for ways to minimize the time necessary to adequately meet your happy needs somewhere where the state flows, you can never be a jack of all trades. This is not to say that you shouldn't push and challenge yourself but it is to say – that you cannot live life doing the things that drain your energy. When you are in flow it is easy to tackle challenges and do the hard things. Find and tap into your flow state.

CHAPTER THREE

SOAR – YOU ARE ENOUGH AND ABLE

The feeling of not being enough is one of the biggest disasters to humanity.
The only way out of this fear
is to acquire as much information and courage as you
can on what you want to embark on. Informed people are courageous. The
more you dare to do something is the more you know, and the more you
know, the more
confident you are to step out with vigor to attempt bigger and exciting things

You Are Enough. A Kiss Gave Me a New Realization

I have heard many tales of people & books about the first kiss. Of course, almost with the same *ooze-de Jeez!* Unlike many of those experiences I have heard shared, mine was a normal feel but I later found an awakening one. As a young boy, I was so shy and never felt confident enough to speak my thoughts especially to a girl. When I did, I would usually end up shaking and almost wetting my pants, which would mortify me and I would even retreat the more. Actually, at home no one believed I could speak in public. I was so silent and an introvert. Though I had an innate urge to speak and do greater things, the thought of not being enough kept me down. As a result of the violent and abusive life I had experienced in my early life, I grew up believing I was neither smart nor loved even when I was extremely praised.

At 14, I left my mum to scratch the ground for myself. I needed school fees and basic needs. I spent most of the time away doing petty trade and casual work to raise money for my survival (as I narrate in my book; *Winning by Choice*). All this long, I was very shy with a very low self-esteem. I saw myself as a village boy who would take ordinary recognition. The closest I ever got to girls in my adulthood was during classwork. I did not express my intentions to the girls I crushed on as much as I would have loved to till I was about 20.

Even then, I never felt enough. I feared to date corporate girls and approach corporate businesses deals. I felt I was not enough for that league even when my peers would praise me. I exhibited courage on the outside as I crumbled on the inside. It was a façade of sorts.

One day, something changed and it started with a kiss that made me awake. It was at a party of a childhood friend, I never used to dance. Even today I still have a dancing phobia. But that evening, I danced just to fit in. Later after the party, I approached a pretty young lady whom I had known since childhood. Her father was a reverend and as such very revered and feared at the same time. She had left for further studies abroad and later joined the UN for work. Much as I had admired her for all the while, I had never got any closer to making my admirations and intentions known. She commanded more respect than myself.

I don't know what came over me that day but I just got the courage and urge to go and speak to her at depth than ever. One thing led to another and before long I kissed her. But immediately after the prompt kiss, I pulled back feeling so sorry. I thought she was going to unleash her wrath on me. At that moment, I felt guilty of my act.

Instead, she looked at the fearful me and said; "You're a good kisser, Nich. Don't you think you are giving me hard time, we're in the open, I can't revert, I'm shy. I thought you would not know how I felt for you Nich since the days of REC." (Rec is a company I had worked for before some years back). Jeez!

I felt like I had won an Oscar. I was enough and admired this entire long when I felt not. When we left the party, we stopped by my hotel and kissed. Just a kiss, nothing more. That ended up being one of the most amazing turn-around moments of my life about feeling enough. Let alone the feeling of the kiss and her calling me a good kisser (wink) but the realization and relief to know that I was admired was enough for me.

I woke up the next day feeling a whole new reality about myself. If she, Ms. Elegant with all her titles and class thought I was that, then I had a lot of untapped ability. That single realization ended my belief that I was not enough. It radically transformed my resolve to tackle bigger dreams.

My take-home is: you are enough. Stop feeling less of who you are, go on and attract it! Wake up on your shaky legs and write that book, make that call, start that company, date that cutie, dream bigger, fight that challenge, sing that song, go for that audition, plough that garden, bargain for that sale, apply for that job, name it all. Do all you can and desire to do. You are enough. Armed with a belief of reality about how stronger and able you are, you turn a magnet attracting greater attention. It is amazing how a belief, when shifted, can create such a dramatic shift in life. You are enough and you can be where the desires of your heart tell you to be. Follow your intuition, you are enough!

Overcome Fear and the Threat to Fail

2 Timothy 1:7 says; "For God hath not given us the spirit of fear; but of power, and of love, and of a sound mind." I have done consultancy/trainings and business for over a decade. I have had thousands of conversations and real experiences about failure, success, and overcoming the fear of failure. It got me thinking a lot about my battle with the fear of failure and things that have held me back in the past. Look, for more than 5 years back, I wanted to start writing books but I was afraid they might not make meaning in people's lives or make money.

"I am short, not educated, not famous, not even that knowledgeable, who will get interested and read your books," were the voices that would play in my mind repeatedly.

Before beginning consultancy, I doubted whether my knowledge would be valuable or helpful to anyone. I wanted to start trainings but I feared if anyone would attend and subscribe to my trainings. In short, I was in the 'busyness' of fearing to fail. The same doubts came up in every business I did. Now I have learnt to take the first step. Once you put that first foot in the waters the rest becomes a limitless adventurous journey. To those who believe in God, you know very well that when you commit, God provides.

Back to my story, just like many others, I had heard enough failures. I wanted to step out, but I was longing for some kind of assurance that I would be more successful than before. I now wonder if I had waited for the assurance where I would be. Many people ask me what I did to overcome fear for failure, here is how I break it down;

Nothing helps like Changing Your Perception of Failure

As I mentioned earlier on changing perspective, the thing that helped me was that I had to change how I perceived failure. My mentors Bob and Ghalib Salim always advised me to give it a thought of it as being black or white.

After that mentorship and mastery, I assumed that you either failed or succeeded and that there wasn't anything in between. But as my conviction grew stronger, I got another perception. The perception of thinking about it with shades of grey (not the movie). So, in terms of my books and trainings, I initially thought that if thousands of people weren't reading or attending them, I would be a failure (black). If they were reading and subscribing, I would have succeeded (white). But thinking in shades of grey, the only way for any of my books or trainings to be a complete failure was that not a single person ever read or attended— which was impossible of course.

I assumed that even if a single person stopped by and read on the cover either online or a physical store, attended a quarter session of my training or streamed live online any of my trainings, that was a small success, therefore it was a shade of grey. Just having one reader or attendee was not my ultimate goal by any means, but it was enough so that I could say it wasn't a total failure! I hope you get my point. I was intimidated by the big black wall of failure and the tiny bright-white spot of success that I was longing for. Basically, what I realized was that I had this very big goal and, in my mind, if I didn't reach it – everything else was a failure. While it sounds a bit vague and conventional, this mind shift was crucial to me getting over my fear of failure. It was exactly what I needed to take the first step and here I have conducted hundreds of trainings, overcame challenges, written a good number of books and started many businesses. See, seeing things in this grey shade wipes away the darkness that mars the blurry stars whose glitter is often missed.

Learn from Michael Jordan as well.

"I've missed more than 9,000 shots in my career. I've lost almost 300 games. 26 times I've been trusted to take the game winning shot and missed. I've failed over and over and over again in my life and that is why I succeed."

-Michael Jordan

Some time back I had a Skype conversation with an Indonesian buddy about the success of my consulting firm (NBK-Premier Solutions) and transformational learning (Legacy Pearls – Africa) and he was pretty surprised when I said that it had been just a series of failures.

"I can't even tell you all the things I have done wrong with my life and business journey," I said to him and he was shocked. Any or all of them could appropriately be labeled as a failure – but because of what I learned from them, they are direct contributors to my life's success and status today. Because of my failures you are reading this book (wink). I am hesitant to use the word "success" because honestly, there is no way that this book and more of my other books or any of my firms would be where they are had it not been for the numerous and continuous failures, embarrassments and frustrations (called success conventionally) that anger me constructively each day. This constructive anger strengthens my conviction. I am using the word failure to drive a point home.

Many books, speakers and trainers use the Jordan approach to failure and I am pretty sure you too can relate. I can't get enough of it, I really enjoy Michael's perspective on failure. Arguably the best basketball player ever on planet earth, he was cut from the high-school basketball team. To me, that speaks volumes. When he started, he was not very good. Michael chose not to believe that and continued to work at his game; failing, failing, and failing some more failing. But, he must have failed so much that he figured out exactly how to play the game to be better than the rest of the world. In fact, statistics show that he failed more than we read and not only in his basketball career but in other aspects of life as well but I am pretty sure that is why he is a champion. He lives with his MOJO.

For me, part of the process of defeating the fear of failure was making a conscious decision to FAIL. I was so bound up in fear that I wouldn't take a step forward in any direction. All I needed was to take a step. Whether it failed or succeeded didn't matter, I just needed to get past the fear of it. If you are in the situation that I was in, I encourage you to prayerfully look at what God has called you to do and don't be afraid of stepping out. Create a life balance sheet to evaluate and improve your net worth and strength against fear and failure day by day. It is possible.

Create a Life Balance Sheet to Determine Your Net Worth

Well, life is a two way test of humor and sorrow and in the intersection is where real happiness is found. There are times when life gives you reasons to laugh and to cry. When we get lost in finding happiness other than meaning, we end up losing the balance. When we get taken over by sorrow, we lose track of our joy.

To overcome this blur of life, one must create a balance sheet. Like in business, a life balance sheet will give you a snapshot of how you're doing in life. We all know what a balance sheet looks like. You have two columns, one holds your assets and the other your liabilities. Assets are items that can provide a future value or benefit. Liabilities, are those things which will create an obligation in the future. Life sometime demands you to be put on a balance sheet.

In business, assets include items such as cash at hand, bank accounts, stocks, bonds. Liabilities include credit card, debt, unpaid bills, mortgage, loans etc. If you subtract liabilities from assets, you get your financial net worth. When your assets are equal to your liabilities, you have a net worth of positivity. If your assets are less than your liabilities, you have a negative net worth. Lastly, if your assets are greater than your liabilities, you have a positive net worth called surplus wealth.

Sometimes if not all, you have to follow a similar model to create a balance sheet of life. In this case, your life assets include all those things which add value to your life and which will allow you to build a brighter future for yourself and your loved ones and the world you live in. They include: knowledge, positive relationships, skills, positive habits, credentials, positive character traits, positive emotions, good health and purpose.

Going to the side of liabilities, list your life liabilities. Your life liabilities are all those things which decrease your ability to lead a good life. They are those things that limit your potential. You might have heard it said of people for example; "He would be a professional footballer had he not become a drug addict." Such statements exist in our everyday life and this means someone built more liabilities than assets. I have been there myself. There are times I struggled with habits that were increasing my liability sheet. The liabilities of a life differ from time to time and can be turned into assets if well observed. As we talked from the start of this chapter, you can shake up things and transform but let's look into those liabilities; they include among others; negative habits, lack of credentials, lack of knowledge, toxic relationships, lack of skills, negative character traits, negative emotions, health problems, lack of purpose.

Determine Your Net worth Now

Just like with your balance sheet, if you subtract your life liabilities from your life assets you'll get your net worth. In this case, a life net worth. Going back to the financial balance sheet example, if your financial net worth isn't what you would like it to be, then you would look for ways to increase your assets and decrease your liabilities. But what if you're not happy with your life's net worth? What can you do to increase it?

Fortunately, there are many things you can do.   In comparison, having a high financial net worth means that you have more money to spend on than the things you want. It also means you have more security, and that you can take advantage of more investment opportunities. A high life net worth, likewise, comes with many benefits. Here are some of them; you'll be happier and happiness is the new productivity tool today. You'll be in a better position to achieve your goals. You'll be in a better position to help others, especially your loved ones. Your life journey will be a lot more pleasant with a high life net worth.

What's your life net worth? How do you plan to increase it?

CHAPTER FOUR
THE FINANCIAL MOJO

*"Struggle without a commensurate financial compensation or reward
is not an indication of an
existing curse on one's life as it is erroneously and
popularly believed, it's just an indication of gross mismanagement of
one's talents and inner resources"*

– Praise George.

The finance magnetism – Alpha of all

As earlier shared, I've had to swim against various tides at different stages of my life. At one time my companies were in debts amounting to over USD 15,000 (too much money for ordinary Ugandan start-ups) yet I also had consumer debts that had equally accumulated to almost 10,000 dollars. There was no way I could keep my mojo on when in such a situation. I would wake up worried of how I was going to make it through. I had a number of pending payments for work I had done. I thought they would be coming through every other day. Following up on those payments was becoming another fulltime job. It's from this that I got a lot of passive and active mentoring from Jason and Ghalib respectively on how to regain a financial mojo.

I may not have attained financial freedom yet but I see a brighter future ahead. When you lose your financial mojo, everything of your life gets to drains. You lose the spark. You struggle to make up with the simple things in life like having a genuine laughter or stand with confidence. It is such a rough pill to swallow that's why very few people can get over it. To be called a bad debtor or a cheat are words you rather have used in reference to you. Not that you are a financial outlaw or dishonest creature but getting back on course is equally as hard. It's difficult in such situations to look into the future and understand just what your life will look like, your patience will always be questioned.

Get me well here, a financial mojo is not to mean being wealthy with huge sums of money but rather the ability to attract financial peace into your life. I remember some time when my girlfriend and I were hit by a financial fall, we were on the edge of falling off the cliff until we finally committed to the process of recovery. It was hard to imagine a life without worry for rent and groceries, school fees and other needs. As I said in the past chapters, it's of great importance to look back and celebrate the small wins and have enabling beliefs. I am certainly not rich, not debt free or immune to financial failures and mistakes but I celebrate the few steps I have taken.

But how is it that other people have been able to get out of situations where others haven't? Well, they're not any special. I have registered a few small wins after climbing such a rugged cliff. It all began when I decided to commit to the recovery process till the end. Seriously! That's all it takes.

Everybody wants to know what the secret is for keeping this rare-to-find mojo burning in a hot potato economy. You have to be willing to do what it takes to follow the process to completion. I have always told my mentees; all of the things we desire in life are not too farfetched. They are not already made available but they are available for the making and are achievable! In fact, if one commits to the making, they arrive closer to experience unknowingly with ease and I can tell you; It's awesome! Each person has their own vision for what they want their life to look like. In most cases, it takes money to get there and this is the critical purpose of this chapter to talk the financial mojo and how to regain it in case things get bad.

What's the Vision?

Here below is a simple exercise I would like to share with you. It will only take a few minutes: Close your eyes. Look at the balance sheet of your life. Do you live in a rat race? If you do, how do you think you can jump out of it? What do you want your financial life to look like by this time next year, three years, five years? What do you want your life to look like 5 years from now? What do you want your life to look like 10 years from now? What do you want your life to look like at retirement? Be as detailed as you can. These questions are meant to streamline your thought process. They are supposed to give you a projection of the future you want. To get that accomplished, you've got to put that in words. That is your vision. Write it down.

Well, it's not easy as typed here, but the **number one** financial mistake that I still make and repeatedly made for so many years and which I see most people making is simply a failure to plan and commit to the plan. Many of us fail to plan for our lives. And when we do, we find reasons to make it ineffective. In her book; *Corporates at a Crossroads*; Joan Mugenzi talks of how people—like organizations— should always set five-year strategic plans. This is key, but few of us consider it. Because of that failure, it's incredibly easy to end up living mediocre lives day by day, month by month and year by year till your face grows wrinkles.

It is so excruciating having countless years of struggle to put food on the table yet the universe sees a reservoir of resources, a genius and hero in you. I have been there. The feeling is not the one you could wish to have given a chance, and there comes having little or no savings to fund emergencies like sickness, community emergency contributions or disaster bills. This steals away your confidence and inner joy.

For the past one year, I have published lots of content on different topics but not finance because I never considered myself qualified. I had no courage of talking about money till I was challenged by the very people I had advised. See, freedom is 80% courage and 20% tactics, so courage is crucial even if the tactics and results may still be lacking but that doesn't stop you from taking the first step.

I believe that having a solid plan and budget for your every move makes all the difference in your finances. Making excuses not to budget is in itself a terrible act. You cannot plan without a budget remember, so it's better to know how to overcome these common excuses that eat us up. I can't recall how many times I have had these excuses. Be informed that budgeting is spiritual.

> *Proverbs 27:23; "Know well the condition of your flocks, and give attention to your herds"*

What I Know For Sure; Budgeting Is Boring:

Sure, we all know budgeting is not cool at all. But what's better; Being frustrated financially and letting your leaks drain away your freedom? Or being proactive and exercising total control over your finances? Total control sounds better to me!

"I already know what I need," you may say. If you're one of those people who say you can keep track of everything in your head, then you're deceiving yourself. Unless you have supernatural powers (which I highly doubt) then you only have a general idea of where your money is going. A solid, zero based budget shows you how to spend your money on paper before you spend it in the real world, I wish I had mustered this practice way back then.

"I hate calculating numbers," is another excuse of all time. I can't tell how many times I held to this excuse to the extent of coming close to patenting or copywriting it as my own invention. But, look; it's just simple addition and subtraction! Don't let this lame excuse keep you stressed about money because you're not a numbers person. Overcome the fear, use a calculator, and learn to get your finances on track for good. If you are in business drop the *I can do it all* mentality, hire someone skilled at record keeping and numbers. They will help you become better. It's until I woke up one day that I saw some few baby steps happen from my fall (I narrated at the beginning). I guess you have seen many rich lads turn down spending on some occasions, they have a budget they stick to and will not run to emergencies that are not too urgent and important. Often times, the people you expect to be raining cash at fundraisings are mute not because they are broke but because of budget constraints. They help and do charity massively but out of budget.

"I keep track of my spending," Congratulations! That's great! Keeping track of your spending is a good start. It shows that you're willing to take the time to develop a regular habit. However, the problem with keeping track of your spending is that it only shows what you've done in the past. A good zero-based budget, done at the beginning of the month, **before** you spend, allows you to be proactive instead of reactive. It provides **direction on how to spend your money instead of showing you how it got spent**. Planning your spending in advance, using a budget, is always better than figuring out what you spent on in the past, after potential damage may have already been done.

"I am always busy I don't have the time," Really? Can't you spare a few minutes a month for something worth your life's joy? C'mon! It's true that it takes longer when you first get started on budgeting as a habit because you're doing something new. Yet even then, it is still possible. The activity is not necessarily time consuming, it's an attitude adjustment. It is not easy like any other task for profit yet the effort and patience later pay off wholesomely.

What I've learned from Making Excuses

I know, from personal experience, what it is like to make excuses when I need to change something in my life. 2012 was my first time ever to be hit by a strong financial fall. I was a collector and supplier of metal scrap; from the slums to factories. At the same time, I was mentoring and empowering ghetto youth.

I was supplying this sorted and packaged scrap to steel recycling firms. It was a capital-intensive business that involved a bigger chain of operators from collectors, transporters, loaders and buyers. It was a profitable venture that I had immersed myself wholly. One season things changed and we lost millions of money. Next was frustration and flunking. Together with colleagues we languished in pain of the losses we had made. There was no redemption until I decided to move on. I started afresh. There is no problem in going back to the drawing board.

I've outgrown the habit of making excuses. I've learned to dive in head first much more quickly than I once did. I still battle with habits of making excuses but at least I can now identify them. I use the five second rule which I mentioned in my book *Winning by Choice* as originally learnt from Mel Robins' book. If you want to change, you'll get past all the lame excuses and dive in head first. Action. Without beating around the bush, a budget saves you from spending more than you make. It allows you to have a ***proactive*** plan for your money, instead of a ***reactive*** one of; "where did all the money go?" It also allows you to have complete control over your money whether big or small, whether you're a student trying to save up from up keep or a great earner, instead of letting money control you, learn to control it. Additionally, commitment to planning and budgeting helps you achieve more ***peace of mind*** about your finances because you have a plan and you are confident about it.

> *One thing you need to know about budgeting is that it's easy, but not at first.*

Budgeting Is Like Riding a Bicycle

Just like when you're learning to ride a bicycle, you end up with scratches, bruises, muscle aches and a few tears because you are likely to fall. At the time of our growing up, it was next to impossible missing out on the fall in the learning process. But once you get the grasp of it you can go anywhere on it joyfully! When you first start doing a budget, it's frustrating and it takes time. When I had just started budgeting, it was hard. It didn't seem to work that well and no one around me including my in-house family liked it. Some actually, at one time, saw it as an act of being stingy, why would I be that calculative? To some it looked as an act of being mean. I swallowed the pain and mockery and stuck to it. But the more I did it, the better I got. And the more my financial discipline bettered. I started regaining some fresh on the bones.

Now I only spend a few minutes a month after my dinner or evening coffee on my budgets. At this point it's pretty much automatic. But if you are new to it, keep in mind that it won't happen overnight. So be patient, stick to the plan and eventually you'll start seeing the awesome fruits of your labor.

The most bragging rich gang and motivational speakers will disappoint you with saying that you need to eat and buy what you want with ease anywhere anytime but don't be fooled, this starts with a budget. Freedom starts with planning, it's not accidental.

Start an Envelope System and Budget with Cash

Call me traditional but unless you are transacting in millions of dollars per day, then you can apply the envelope system. It is the best way to stay confident with money and life needs. If you consistently have trouble knowing where all your money goes then using an envelope system (along with a detailed budget) will get you on the right track.

One of the problems I faced when I was in deep debt and which I guess all people face as well is that they don't have complete knowledge about how much they spend. The result is that they spend more than they make month after month. This is how one ends up in debt unknowingly. Doing this for years on end eventually results in huge amounts of debt and a financial stunted growth. This is how I personally ended up in debt.

Practice is what separates the top achievers from mediocres.

Envelopes can be just documented envelopes or accounts.

Pay Your Bills

Most people don't normally pay cash for their utility bills until they are due. This brings about panic and temptation to borrow an emergency consumer debt. Pay your bills, that's envelope number one. Even if you do not have a consistent cash flow, still, consider every first money earned to be paid for consumer bills.

Identify and fill Envelopes

Once you know which budget categories you want to use cash for during the month, label each one with a specific category. Envelopes can be a written list to keep track and discipline you by committing to it as a law you don't need to break. Next, add up all those categories and get a grand total of how much cash you will need to put in your envelopes. Then fill each envelope with the amount designated in your budget. Once you have the correct amount of money in each envelope, you can start spending that money as you need it throughout the month.

By the way, it's not of any harm if you even use real envelopes for starters; look foolish and old till you build the habits.

Do Not Steal From Your Envelopes

If one of your envelopes runs out of money, you might be tempted to steal from another, please don't. This usually happens when things are tight. However, stealing from yourself won't be of help no matter the excuse, it will soon catch up with you. No stealing. Discipline is the key in all, the situation won't be long.

If you have a non-monthly bill you pay every 3 or 6 months, such as car loan, you can split that bill into monthly increments and place it in an envelope. For instance, if your vehicle loan is UGX 450,000 every three months, then put UGX 150,000 each month into an envelope labeled "Car loan". When it's time to pay that bill you have the money available in it full without having to fidget. Congratulations, you now have an envelope system set!

Emergency Funds: Lessons from My Mother

After the budgeting discipline, one needs to work on having an emergency fund. This is something you'll need to do before you even start paying off debt. A number of people don't have enough savings to cover a UGX 500,000 (100-150 USD) emergency. I have been there a thousand times.

That's just crazy and it keeps one rotating about unhappily in a rat race. Well in this *gig* [1] economy, it may be hard to outgrow the situation but gradually you can reduce the frustration. And it's just one reason why so many people have their backs against the wall financially. I can't tell how many times I borrowed and still do for emergencies. Ever since I learnt this, I have drastically reduced on the rate. And Boy! You can't know the freedom attached to that. Buy me coffee and I tell you about this, hehe!

An emergency fund is absolutely the sweetest *bae* to date, so essential to a happy life and good financial plan because it keeps you from going into a panic mode and making financial decisions that you would regret later. An available emergency fund always is the best thing any champion can have. It gives you a peace of mind. You know you can cover an emergency when it comes up. What if you lose your job or business sales or gigs? An emergency fund will keep the bills paid until you can find your next gig.

My mother was so particular when it came to saving. She was a subsistence farmer who grew millet. Whenever our millet was harvested, mother would first set aside bundles of millet which was for sowing the following season. Another bundle would be given away to friends and family. She would reserve another portion and keep it for the future. She would keep it away in a special granary and another portion for daily use till the following season. I didn't know why she always did all this. I wondered why she didn't just keep all the millet in one granary since it was all ours.

I came to learn all this later in life when I was grappling with financial challenges. Even though my mother had hugely mastered the saving culture, we didn't understand it as children. Maybe we thought her ways were outdated and traditional, and it became and still is a hard task to muster at times. On the brighter side, with the different ways of saving for emergencies and the future, she taught us to find an option that suites us perfectly.

I have come to realize why she did all this (I wish I understood it early enough those days). I have learnt from her ways and designed tips that can help one manage their resources better. In whatever she did, mother always made a budget and stuck to it. For the budgeting to be successful, she used to start by keeping track of all monthly expenses. This helped us get a rough idea of what to spend on during a given month. She wasn't technical while doing this. She used estimates and she was comfortable with that. In reality, once you have the monthly estimates written down, you become very objective and only take down the stock of what you actually spent. One financial expert says;

> When writing your actual budget, you also need to consider your spending history in order to come up with a projected budget. When preparing a budget, it is very important to be true to yourself.

Spending wisely

Earning less than two dollars per week, my mother used to spend not only wisely but innovatively. In order to experience food and financial freedom in a poor and domestic violent home, mother taught us to get off the "consumption treadmill". One mistake we normally make is selling tomorrow's gold in exchange of today's silver worries. Try as much as possible to avoid the habits of borrowing tomorrow's expected income to meet today's expenditures if you want to have emergency fund available. Many times I borrowed from people expecting to earn and pay the following day only to be disappointed and fail to pay back. This drove me to losing friends' trust sometimes.

Broadening the Mind

My mother had no formal education yet she was self-sustaining. She learnt through attending community workshops. In modern age it is easier and vital to educate your mind on the different ways to increase your savings through reading. Dedicate a few hours each week to reading books and see the effect they'll have on you.

Rewarding Thyself

My mother had concrete fact-based goals when saving. Every time she achieved her set goals, she would reward herself and her family for the achievements. Saving for emergencies or anything does not mean that you have to live as a miser. Even in tough times, my mother wouldn't miss buying for us fish or clothing after a successful market day or crop season. When you learn to reward yourself even in the smallest you have achieved, it means you are creating a pool of motivation and power that will propel you ahead for greater goals.

How Can You Build an Emergency Fund?

Believe me, you'll gain incredible peace of mind when you're able to pay cash in a crisis like health issues or death of loved ones. One of the first places to start is with your budget (I am not sorry to bring the word budget again). Most people find that when they start writing down a budget, they find hundreds of cash a month that was being wasted. Start putting that money into your emergency fund. Also, you can find ways to make extra money. There are plenty of ways to get an emergency fund together when you put your mind to it and get creative.

Get Out Of the Mess and Live Free

The reason we struggle is because we refuse to do the right now waiting for the perfect time which never comes. What we don't realize is that the more we delay starting, the more difficult it becomes.

For the sake of this chapter let's focus on financial messes like debt and brokenness. Ask anybody that's out of debt or trying to get out and they will tell you it's the best thing ever did financially. Having no debt brings freedom and peace of mind, you just can't get freedom when you owe people money.

Wishing As You Swing in Your Chair Doesn't Work

Debts can be paid off. All it takes is the will. The will is backed up by a plan. The plan contains your day to day steps to alleviate the problem. Raising the money, praying hard and all may not sustain you for long if you do not have a plan. This rarely works; I speak this with confidence. You ought to come up with a road map for you to follow lest you go back to the ways of old. And worse of it is you have no plan when an emergency arises next. But when it's time to get out, flying by the seat of your pants just doesn't work. It is very easy to revert to old habits after a few weeks or months, making little to no progress.
So, what do you do?

Be Mad, Go Naked

You have to be mad enough at the situation to kill it for good. Take one scary step that so many people fail to take when it comes to getting out. It's one of the most logical steps in getting started, yet most people never consider doing it. If they do, it strikes fear in their hearts because it counters to what we're all taught. "What is it?" You must be asking? That thing that you *must* do is to 'go naked'. Sounds scary and shameful, right? I don't mean you abandon your clothes, you will be arrested for crimes against the mighty Anti-pornography Act.

What I mean by going naked is to get rid of your habits and practices and don't take on any new situation that leads to debt or stagnancy ever again. You will ask, then how will I survive? Take a debt only when you must and calculate the risks. Act strong not emotionally. Break some rules. Be honest with your debtors and ask for some time to avoid the pressure of having to borrow to pay another debt. It is not easy but gradually it is mustered if decided on. If you have been indebted, keep it in mind that it won't be a one day thing. You will have to reduce day by day. If you have survived on lies, (which is a common practice among the indebted), you won't reduce lying in a day's time, you just have to drop on the number of lies day by day. It may sound funny but it works.

Going Naked In Public Is Uncomfortable

Public nakedness is, by far, an act of shame upon one.

That is why, it is kept as a preserve for one in their privacy. Walking around the neighborhood naked can make you feel uncomfortable and vulnerable. Going naked with no coin or worse without any hope of getting any is hell on earth. We have been conditioned to think that we need money to fit in society. We've been told that if we don't have money on us, we could end up in a financial disaster. When you cut yourself out of such beliefs and practices and decide you'll never go back, you actually become more liberated financially than you've ever been. You have to accept that you have no money till you earn it.

   "Start by doing what's necessary; then do what's possible; and suddenly you are doing the impossible" - Francis of Assis

Awareness Of Situations

Accept that you are in debt, accept the embarrassments of it - be content with the truth but mad about it, and draw plans to get over. Draw a Budget. A proper budget allows you to never spend more than you make and get complete control over your money. Period.

Don't Be Irrational; Pay Yourself First

Just like losing weight, freedom is all about establishing good habits for a lifetime. Going back to credit cards, borrowing for emergencies and no written budget will only get you right back where you were. So, don't get stupid and erase what you've achieved! First, you have to understand that when you get paid, your priority should be to pay yourself first before you pay your bills. When it comes down to it, your first responsibility is to you and your family (if you have), so your money should reflect that. Actually, Christians recommend paying yourself second after returning the tithe. Most people tend to take the opposite approach. You pay the bills and hope you have enough left over to put some money in savings if you're lucky. At that point you're putting yourself last and jeopardizing your financial future because of it.

Be Like the Heart, Guard Yourself Selfishly

Do you know the story of the heart? The heart selfishly keeps more of the good blood to itself because it knows that the survival of all other parts depends on it and its survival as well depends on the health of other parts. Reward yourself generously from the labour of hands so that whatever springs out of you is of good cheer. So learn to irrigate your grounds first before any other thing. All the other expenses can wait.

Invest

It doesn't matter how strong you are, it's until you do something that the strength can be realized. Start with what you can, what you have and where you are, you are stronger than you realize.

Investing is a wide and complicated subject that you could need a book of its own. There is no ultimate knowledge of it. I believe that's why a large number of people including myself never started investing easily. Start learning everything you can about investing. The goal is not to become as knowledgeable as a professional but the more you know the better off you'll be. When it comes to investing, patience and consistency pay off. You're not going to get rich overnight. But when you consistently put your money into investments month after month, year after year, they will be the springs from which you can always drink.

Have Fun without Spending a Lot of Money

It's great to have a cash envelope for entertainment in your budget. In my recovery, I set aside a small portion for it in my own budget every month. I began by enjoying the free fun; going to the library, taking random walks or a hike. If you're looking for free events, do a Google search for free events in your city and see what's available, I recommend *Eventbrite*. With time, you can go out for movies or other forms of entertainment which are within your means.

Do a No Spend Challenge

Lately, doing a no spend challenge has become a popular thing. It can take any form you want. The gist is that you spend no money on a particular activity or item that can be outlived for a certain amount of time. The result is that you save money and form new habits in the process.

Visualize

If you have a goal in mind like saving for a down payment on your dream house or having a certain amount in your retirement accounts by a certain date, make it visual. Create a visual board. I talk about this in detail in the second and third chapter of my book *Winning by Choice*. You can visually represent your goal to see whether the progress you're making works great. It's all about engaging the senses and having a constant reminder of where you stand so you'll stay motivated to reach your goal.

CHAPTER FIVE

FEEL ALIVE AMIDST ALL

*Most of us that have ever struggled financially, emotionally, spiritually
or in any other aspects of life
were as a result of under-utilizing the inner resources. Money does not
guarantee success. A well planned vision does.*

Escape the Miserable-rat race swiftly

Using a quick explanation, a rat race is an endless, self-defeating, or pointless pursuit. It takes the image of a caged rat in a laboratory trying to run around. I use the term 'miserable-rat race' to refer to the rat race of unhappiness and lack of abundance in life. I write this chapter from my perspective.

Not everyone is called to be an entrepreneur but it is pretty clear to me that this is a part of who I am created to be. So, for those of you in a situation like mine, or want to join I hope this helps.

In my early 20s, I eagerly wanted to work. However, the idea of corporate employment never convinced me. When my friends began working in the corporate world, they wore good neckties and I envied them. It didn't take long before I realized that conventional employment was not for me, not only for not having a college degree but I didn't resonate with it.

To me, the compound care guys, the janitors and drivers outside these cool offices demonstrated that my friends were locked up in a cage while others had to work outside freely, happy and with enough room to break conventional rules. Don't judge me. That was my perspective at the time. The saddest part was seeing so many of them who were curious, daring to change the world, creative and risk averse, who had dreams of things they wanted to do working long hours in jobs they hated. A number of them were eaten up by the urge to grow which seldom come through. Rather than take a chance on realizing their dreams, they settled to become "lifers" on jobs they did not enjoy.   The problem is that each day my friends saw themselves looking more and more like some of those around them in offices and this is what makes it look like a miserable-rat race. Employment is ok, you can do better and change the world with it but being in a job you hate is the number one miserable-rat race one can be in.

One day while meditating, I thought of what I would be like in 20 years' time. I wanted to be a teacher. My version of teaching was training and sharing unconventional wisdom for transformation (which I do now at Legacy Pearls Africa). I wanted something so different for my life, made by my own rules, but looking from that perspective I was on the wrong track to get there, and there is nothing more I defined as a miserable-rat race more than being on a job one hated.

I have been working for myself for the last 15 years. I have both an opportunity and obligation to make things, live life and handle risk my way. Much as at times it hurts, I still enjoy my falls because they get me off the maze quickly. I am glad I followed my heart. This is not in any way meant to downplay the effort that many put in at their places of work, not at all. It is about what makes you happy and feel alive regardless of the money or status.

You know what your heart desires, do not be caged when you can freely sing and fly. Go for what your heart timely feels for no matter what.

Doing Something Out Of Love

I always endeavor to do the things I want. I enjoy figuring out how to manage my time and other resources to use them in the service of others. I like breaking rules and making my way off the conventional ways. I enjoy defying the status quo. I think it is important to mention that I don't write books and train because I think it would be a profitable venture. I write because I enjoy it. I have been advised by a number of people that I should do something I love doing and find a way to get paid for it or after it. Often, it takes some time before one may earn from doing what they love. The rules are changing and now more than ever the possibilities of doing what you love and get paid are endless.

At the time when I was trying ways to generate income, I tried many things that failed. I still have a lot that fail. Majority of them failed because I realized that I didn't really enjoy them. Most of them were making money, but I realized that it wasn't something I wanted to do, so why keep doing it?

Starting a business, career, relationship or anything should be cheap, easy and fun. The businesses I have started with ease and fun have always flourished; **Legacy Pearls - Africa**, **NBK-Premier solutions** and **Agrimax Valleys** and soon **Legacy Pearls Academy & DETT Uni-learning** (online learning platforms) **and DETT Fest** have all been businesses I started with less than 100 dollars and with much fun. The days of having to risk a lot of joy, energy and time to start on a career or dream are gone.

Starting Something with a Winning Mantra against Failure

It took me years to take this step. I was in business but petty trade for lack of words to use. Then I finally realized that I needed to start something bigger with a mind that I would win. And that if it failed, at least I would have tried meaning I would have less regrets. I had to overcome my fear of failure because it was paralyzing me as I narrated in the second chapter. I found myself spending way too much time trying to figure out the perfect plan even before I took the first step. The amazing thing is that as I started taking steps, the plan became clearer. My point is that the rat race is just like a horizon line, it stays the same until you start walking towards it. As you get closer, you see things that you couldn't see before.

In relationship, I was too much of a planner than an executer that no progress was registered ever. It was like trying to map out each step of a hike on a rugged hill that I have never climbed. I finally decided to hike. Just get going.

I Decided To Start

In 2009, I started my metal scrap collection business. My first financial goal was to multiply my UGX 8000 (3.5 dollars then) capital by 1000 times in the first year. I gave myself 6 months to realize it. By reaching that goal, I would be inspired to keep going. Successfully achieving goals is one of the most motivating things out there to overcome the rat race. That's why I worked hard to set attainable goals. I was only able to hit the mark in the eighth month. But since I had set myself a target, it gave me a chance to go for it.

Lowering Expectation to a Reasonable Point

Handling risk is part and parcel of life. Some people try (unsuccessfully) to remove any form of all risk from their life while others seem not to take risk into consideration when making any decisions. It's important for one to always consider taking the risk. I knew that stepping into entrepreneurship had many elements of risk only that I did not know how diverse they were. I had to learn cutting my coat according to my cloth. I had not given as much thought as I needed to the circumstances that befell me.

I find risk to have a high resonance with expectations. When you consider the risk involved in whatever you are doing, your expectations are equally checked. You cannot have high expectations without a thought of risk. In a fight, you always expect your opponent to hit you anywhere. You know you are probably going to get punched in the stomach and it will hurt either way, but if you are prepared for it, it won't be as bad.

Feel Fully Alive As Much As Possible

A few months ago, I watched the movie *The Mountain between Us*. The story is an awakening of life amidst adversity and hopelessness to become the champion one is called to be. The two main characters get stranded at a mountain top following a plane crash. After days of waiting, they realize no help is coming through. They decide to descend the mountain in faith that help will come. They have no idea where they are let alone or where they are headed. Their chances of surviving keep dwindling by every passing minute. They are convinced they are going to die on the mountain. Drawn together by the situation, they fall in love while descending the mountain. After all hardships and commitment at the end they both survive. But one thing that caught my attention is the affection that grows between the two. Much as they were stuck, they felt fully alive to fall in love.

To feel fully alive and in love when near death? To feel fully alive when their lives were in jeopardy? In comparison to our daily lives, we all have mountains to climb down, we all face some crushes and find ourselves in places we know less about. Through all the daily routine of life, let's not forget to feel alive.

Wonderful moments in life do not stay for long. It occupies a smaller percentage. Those who dare to celebrate that percentage are the champions we celebrate. Those who are always very alive as much as possible amidst all. Everybody needs those moments that move you and stir your soul. They are very available only that we run away from the door that would take us there. Life demands your heart to sing for joyfulness always. Like in the movie, this happens by taking passionate risks. By moving out of your comfort zone or doing things you didn't think you would, you learn to feel alive for every moment of your life. Life is short and you deserve to be alive. So, let your heart sing. Be bold and take some risks.

CHAPTER SIX

IN THE SKY OF ABUNDANCE

*"I have come to accept the feeling of not knowing where
I am going. And I have trained myself to love it. Because it is only when we
are suspended in mid-air with no landing in sight, that we force our wings
to unravel*

*and alas begin our flight. And as we fly, we still may
not know where we are going. But the miracle is in the
unfolding of the wings. You may not know where you're going, but you know
that so long as you spread your wings, the winds will carry you to some
destination".*

— *C. Joy Bell C.*

Keeping Afloat

Find peace and courage in the troubled seas. Don't let a hard lesson harden your heart. Hold tightly to your dream while at the same time opening your heart and mind to new ideas and experiences.

It's when you have ventured into something new that you grow stronger and more capable. You must hold tightly to your dream with an open mind and heart. These may be a bunch of pain, adventures or worry but they are worth the effort. Your own perspective will become clearer when you look at things from different angles. Think of these pointers; **#1. Say Goodbye to Old You, Say Hello to New You**

Learn to trust the journey. When opportunities and circumstances close their doors on you, it's a hint that your growth rail requires someone/thing different.

Life is simply making room. So, embrace your goodbyes, because every goodbye you receive in life sets you up for an important hello. In everything we do, it's never too late to say goodbye to old beliefs, thoughts or habits so you can get set up for a new hello. Don't measure your success by failures, measure your success by the attempts you have made. Don't stop until you find a way to be and do better. It may not look the way you want it to but make the decision to be determined to do what it takes to press on. Say good bye where need be and embrace new hellos.

#2. Distance Yourself from Approvals

The hardest part of attachment is that you have to give up some of your interests. Of course, it's difficult to distance yourself from someone you care about, a work place you treasured, a title you have been known for, a business you have been known for without getting hurt in the process. But that's just the thing, there's nothing concrete and reliable about these fantasies and they will not build up anything.

The reality of such hurting fantasies, relationships and attachments results and consistent actions has disproven them and shown you their true colors. It's best to believe them and distance yourself and venture into new horizons.

During such times, anger and weariness may have a hold on you. At times of hopelessness, distancing and disconnecting yourself seems to be a better dwelling place than enduring unchanging heartaches.

#3. Follow the Steepest Routes; - With Joy

Do the hard things. Distance yourself from the thought that everything in life should be easy. There are no shortcuts to any place worth going for. Enjoy the challenge of your achievements. See the value in your efforts and be patient with yourself. Enjoy the process more than the destination itself. Dance in the rain like it is shining.

Be patient and resilient. As Mark and Angel says; Realize that patience is not just about waiting, it's the ability to keep a good attitude while working hard on your important goals and dreams. It is the accelerator to feeling fulfilled. You need to do the hard things with joy and passion. Those are the things that ultimately define you. They make the difference between existing and living, between knowing the path and walking it, between a life of mediocrity and a life filled with progress and fulfillment. It's the difference between reality and expectation.

#4. Forgive Even When the Other Party Don't Necessarily Deserve It

Forgiveness is recognizing the reality that situations and events cannot be reversed. There's no point in letting such past event to dominate your life. Forgiveness cleans the slate and enables you to step forward with candor.

See, forgetting the people/situations that hurt you is your gift to them;

forgiving the people/situations that hurt you is a gift to yourself. You forgive not because they necessarily deserved forgiveness but because you deserve a peace of mind going forward.

Keep in mind that some relationships will temporarily split, only to heal and grow back together over time, people change, situations change and today's mistake can become tomorrow's opportunity. Forgive. Forgiveness alone makes this possible, if it's meant to be. Such is the roundness of the world.

#5. Don't Exchange What You Want Most for What's Easiest At The Moment

Well, talking of courage, I am typing this with my heart. I have been there in the gutters and I know what it means to be the punching bag. To attract better outcomes in life, you have to become better on the inside. Yes, you heard me. You have to grow a thick skin and stand strong amidst all odds.

You cannot do the same things and expect different results. You can't blame or count on someone else all the time and make shifts. Take full responsibility for the next step against what has happened.

Start transforming your mindset. Acquire a new skill even when you think it's of less use now, you never know what the future holds. Upgrade your habits and cultivate new relationships at all costs.

Our lives are 10% what happens to it and 90% the choice to deal with what happens. Seriously, don't settle, fight for what you believe in. It is worth the effort!

#6. Deal With the Situations and Thoughts That Worry You

Who would you be, and what would you do more, if you removed the thought/situations that's worry you most? In 2012, I found myself in a work position that worried me. Every day I would bottle up and worry the more. I spent a lot of unnecessary energy worrying, which turned into resentment and anger and less productivity. It left me drained.

One morning, I woke and confronted the fear and moved on to enjoy my work, and indeed work became more fun and smoother for me. This brought me to appreciate the beauty of life; our vulnerability to circumstances and our ability to overcome. You can always choose a mindset that moves you forward and doing so will help you change things from the inside out, and ultimately allow you to grow beyond the struggles you can't control at any given moment.

Everyone has had their share of life. Negative thoughts should not become residents in your mind, they can come but you can deny them influence on you. In life, you trip and fall, make mistakes and fail, but stand strong through it all. Live and learn. It's in your imperfection that your identity as human is defined.

#7. Choose Yourself First

Before you think of being a priority in other people's lives, make yourself one in yours. You too are as important as the others. With some people, it's just difficult to make themselves a priority sometimes.

Too often we put the needs of everyone else ahead of ourselves. Putting others first gives joy but if you don't consider yourself too, you won't sustain the act of putting others first. Choose you, first. Become your own support system. Love yourself instead of simply loving the idea of others loving you. Don't wait to be chosen, choose yourself.

I've learned from life experience that one of the best ways to help you and get more accomplished is by making yourself a priority. If you don't take care of yourself, then you won't be able to take care of others.

With advance in age comes wisdom. I've learned that you can have those around you do more for you only if they see you choosing yourself for worthier causes. You just need to be clearer about what needs to get done. Make yourself a priority today and you will be amazed how magnetic it will be in attracting positive outcomes your way.

#8. Strive To Find Joy In Less

Every day, remind yourself that the richest human isn't the one who has the most rather the one who finds joy in works of their hands. Abundance and prosperity are only but a mindset. Appreciate what you have to be motivated to do more.

Challenge yourself to be less impressed by the material possession, title and fame. Be more impressed by the life you lead. You are incredibly fortunate to be experiencing this moment right here, right now. And the more you appreciate it, the better it will be and the more chances to attract more. Find joy in less.

#9. Say Less When Less Means More. Starve Your Frustrations!

Sometimes, you are as wise as the silence you leave behind. Sometimes, the right words are not words but a heart with intention of good. Walk away from the drama you feel inclined to engage in. Say less when less means more. Live accordingly. Do your best not to judge other people, for you do not know their pain or sorrows or struggles or circumstance at their front.

If you cannot speak a kind word, say nothing at all. Enjoy the inner glow you get from letting go and not engaging in drama.

When you stop doing the wrong, the right things suddenly have a chance to catch up with you. Some people call it the law of attraction.

And as Jose N Harris said:

> There comes a time in your life when you walk away from all the drama and the people, situations, habits and activities that create it. You surround yourself with people and habits that make you laugh. Learn from the bad and focus on the good. Love the people who treat you right and pray for the ones who don't. Life is too short to be anything but happy. Falling down is part of life. Getting back up is living.

Starve your frustrations and feed your motivations.

#10. Say No When You Need To

Saying yes to everything puts you on the fast track to a regretful existence. Feeling like you're constantly busy and overwhelmed is typically the result of saying yes too. We all have obligations, but a healthy, effective pace can only be found by properly managing your yes. So, stop saying yes when you want to say no. You can't always be agreeable; that's how people and situations take advantage of you. Sometimes you have to set clear boundaries.

#11. Be Consistent When Working On Meaningful Goals

One thing that forfeits many of us from showing results despite having good dreams, it's the lack of consistency with which we do what we do.

Consistency is king in every big achievement. A writer betters their craft by writing more often as is with any other craft. When you're looking for a job, do it consistently. Want to lose weight; exercise consistently. Name it all. One thing that many regret is not being consistent with their goals. Lack of consistency creates room for procrastination and giving up.

Let this be our wake-up call!

Consistency brings a level of freedom and opportunity that very few of us realize until we no longer have it. As they say, there are seven days in the week and someday isn't one of them. This minute, hour, day, week, month and year is the right one to act; - a relationship? - act on it today tomorrow and the other day, be consistent. As a business owner market today, tomorrow and the other days, not just once. It takes 100 shots to get one ball in the ring. One action will only result into one time wonders. Consistency is the master key to championship!

#12. Learn How to Handle Expectations

When I was around 15 years, my mother told me a story of the abundance that was about to come if I kept striving. Young as I was, my hopes were aroused. I expected to get into college, have a career after college and that one day I'd meet a nice woman and we would get married and be happy thereafter.

Life was thought to be that simple in my head until reality struck. The universe rolled away the carpet and underneath it all the chaff was unveiled. That's when I claimed and begged to be entwined with resilience and optimism.

Such thoughts were not only unique to me. Many of us carried them around and we still do. Things do not just happen by sitting back and building castles in the air. However, nature has her own way of unveiling herself. Stories change when you move a muscle, when you do something. Life calls you to learn and unlearn along the way, that's how the picture becomes clearer. The things we desire are within reach, all we need is to move away from our comfort and find them. Accept nature, ignore human logic and make a choice to win no matter what. At the end of it all, what will mess you up most in life is the picture in your head of how it is supposed to be and how you handle the reality of making it become real.

#13. Make Time for the Right People

When it comes to relationships and people, you'll just want to be around the few people who make you warm, smile or be encouraged for all the right reasons. Be intentional and spend more quality time with those who help you love yourself more. You cannot give them anything in exchange for that. Make time for them.

Being with them and listening to them with passion and without anticipation of the next event, is the biggest compliment they can receive from you. This helps you to be a priority to them and an influence for better things from them.

#14. Take Care of your Health

Did you know poor health care habits (both emotional and physical) could have a terrible effect on your productivity? Poor nutrition and wellness habits can result in decreased energy levels. No matter how much you think you dislike exercise and healthy eating, your body needs them.

Let not the pursuit of success consume your health. Health is wealth, this you already know. Did you know that recent studies conducted on people who were battling with depression showed that consistent exercise combined with a healthy diet and other practices raises happiness? Yes. Your health matters. Consider it.

You are less likely to relapse if you get good food, exercise in all forms. A higher sense of self accomplishment and self-worth comes from having a good health practice.

#15. Be Relentless. Start Over Again and Again

Ever played any game? At times, to win a game one has to make back moves. Think about how this relates to our lives. Did you have a short fall? Be relentless, start over again and again. Nera! Nera!

At times when it feels like you're running into one dead end after another, it's actually a sign that you need to take a break. Life gradually teaches us that U-turns are allowed. As Denzel Washington said, "Don't confuse movement with progress." So, turn around when you must! There's a big difference between giving up, running wildly and starting over again in the right direction. Promise yourself this day that no matter what the case is, you don't relent. Giving up is cool, the rat race looks busy but the scary part of it is that nothing gets paid at the end.

#16. Don't Be Idle to Judge People

Most, if not all chances are that everybody you meet has their unique set of successes, struggles, weaknesses, achievements and failures. Everybody you will meet is afraid of something, loves something, believes in something and has lost something. Know this. It is natural. There is always much behind the curtain than what you see.

You never know what someone has been through, or what they're going through today. Don't be lazy and make empty judgments about them. Be kind. Observe, learn but don't rush to pass judgment. Seek the truth. Listen; you never know what will be said. Be humble. Be teachable and teach. Don't assume you have nothing to teach the world.

#17. Be a Mentee or a Mentor.

The power of mentorship is incomparable to anything else. Whether your mentor is a kid or an elder, female or male, influential or not; mentorship is mentorship.

A mentor changed my life when I was a teenager. Mentorship is why The Branson's, the Gates and The Jobs are who they are. In my second year at the technical school, I was drifting in the wrong direction. I ended up flunking all the time. I was over ambitious with no direction than to the ruins. As a 16-year-old adolescent, stumbling into things there and here, I found myself burning my head with thoughts and answering less questions.

Then I met a mentor

I was working at a workshop over the evenings to earn extra cash for my stay at school. I couldn't afford myself a decent meal. One day, someone took interest in me and brought me a torn copy of Victor Earl Frankil's book; *Man's Search For Meaning*. Much as it had a few missing pages, it worked in my favor. I was lucky to understand that according to the author, the way a prisoner imagined the future affected his longevity or short-stay in the struggle. That moment changed my life. On top of giving me the book, this old man asked to be my mentor.

This retired educationist began teaching me resilience, consciousness, business and conservative principles. Principles that shaped my new outlook on life journey. Through his help, and the love of my mom (that woman! Blessed be her soul), I got back on track, graduated from school and got my first job. Later, I started my company and another and more and later a college Diploma.

It is because of mentorship that I set my life goals and purpose: to positively affect the lives of people with a message of hope through my books and trainings, entrepreneurship and opportunity identification and sharing.

I can honestly say I'm not certain where my life would have led without mentors. They helped make me the man I am today. I am so grateful for mentorship, nothing comes close. It helped a village boy who grew up rejected and abused to soar and write this book you are reading. This book will awaken the Champion mojo lying within you.

As you come to the end of this book, I congratulate you and I hope you join me in recognizing and celebrating mentorship today. Even the slightest gesture, the smallest amount of time and encouragement or advice can make a difference in someone's life, be a mentor or get mentored. You only live to make a mark when you are mentored or mentoring.

#18. **Living in Surrender State**

Whenever we talk of surrender and letting go, most people think I am contradicting myself on the resilience and persistence gospel I preach. But no. Surrender is not about giving up, handing power over, or failing. It is not waving the white flag of defeat. It isn't. Surrender is the beautiful space of acceptance. It's that arms-wide-open energy that is deeply rooted in trust of transcendence. Surrender is knowing that even though things might not seem perfect or to be moving according to plan that everything will turn out just the way it's meant to be for the good.

> *Surrender is how we get out of our own way and let the universe bend reality to our side.*

This is how we experience a life of real freedom. Free from limiting self-beliefs, emotional blocks, and negative self-talk. Surrender allows us to step into our lives and be. We learn to embrace the good, the bad, and the ugly— with an open heart. It's from this place that peace is nurtured.

Letting go is one of the hardest but best decisions one learns to make along the way. Leaving behind unanswered questions and painful memories when life demands so, getting over a missed opportunity, leaving behind regrets and anger. It is all hard. Letting go is being in position to surrender. We yearn for the significant other who walked away from us, instead of considering the person who's been next to us. We wish for the missed opportunity to visit us again than an opening of doors right in front of us. We let these moments in life weigh us down, making our hearts heavier by the day. We let pain consume us, making us look past the positive occurrences in our lives. We let the past take control of our present and future, making us miss out on the high of life. We need to muster the art of surrender if not for anyone, for the sake of ourselves.

Surrender brings back the serenity and peace in our lives, something we lost along the way. Surrendering and letting go are not an end in themselves, they are only a means. It is building bridges to new and better beginnings. Rather, it remains perfect through continuous rebirth.

Through awareness, personal growth, and intuition we can invite surrender in when it comes knocking. It's a choice made in the present moment. Seeing reality for what it is and opening up to it wholeheartedly. It's from that rich territory of surrender that we finally let go of the limiting energy of control and force. And when we aren't controlling, we have completely stepped out of our own way. We are ready to receive; to tap into the abundant possibilities available to us, and to manifest a life free from restraint and restrictions. Energy flows where attention goes. Surrender!